THE
LENAPE
INDIANS

THE JUNIOR LIBRARY OF
AMERICAN INDIANS

THE
LENAPE
INDIANS

Josh Wilker

CHELSEA JUNIORS

a division of CHELSEA HOUSE PUBLISHERS

FRONTISPIECE: Ohtas, a wooden Doll Being that was said to bring the Lenapes prosperity and good health.

CHAPTER TITLE ORNAMENT: A carved wooden mask of a *mesingw*, or game spirit, worn by a dancer in the Big House ceremony.

Chelsea House Publishers
EDITORIAL DIRECTOR Richard Rennert
EXECUTIVE MANAGING EDITOR Karyn Gullen Browne
COPY CHIEF Robin James
PICTURE EDITOR Adrian G. Allen
ART DIRECTOR Robert Mitchell
MANUFACTURING DIRECTOR Gerald Levine
PRODUCTION COORDINATOR Marie Claire Cebrián-Ume

The Junior Library of American Indians
SENIOR EDITOR Ann-Jeanette Campbell

Staff for THE LENAPE INDIANS
COPY EDITOR Nicole Greenblatt
EDITORIAL ASSISTANT Joy Sanchez
ASSISTANT DESIGNER John Infantino
PICTURE RESEARCHER Sandy Jones
COVER ILLUSTRATOR Hal Just

7 9 8 6

Library of Congress Cataloging-in-Publication Data

Wilker, Josh.
The Lenape Indians / Josh Wilker.
  p. cm. — (The Junior library of American Indians)
Includes index.
Summary: Examines the history, culture, and future prospects of the Lenape (also known as the Delaware) Indians.
ISBN 0-7910-1665-X
      0-7910-2029-0 (pbk.)
1. Delaware Indians—Juvenile literature. [1. Delaware Indians.
2. Indians of North America.] I. Title. II. Series.   93-8719
E99.D2W457 1994   CIP
973'.04973—dc20   AC

CONTENTS

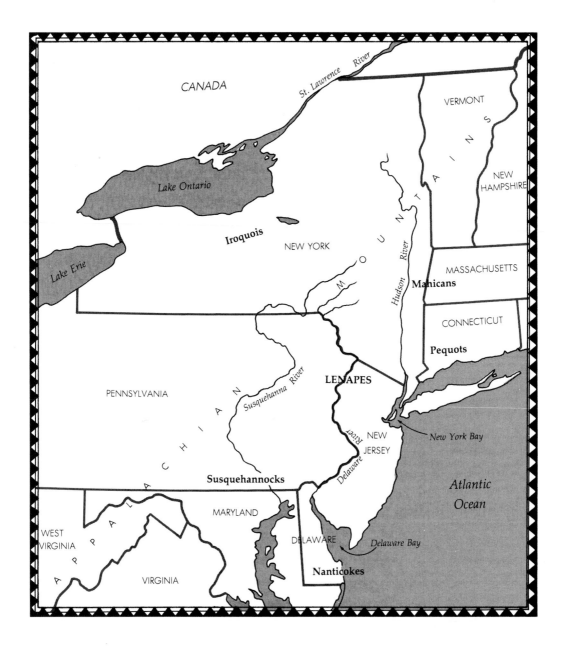

The Lenapes inhabited what is today southern New York, New Jersey, eastern Pennsylvania, and Delaware. Somewhere in the woods of this territory the three lost boys encountered the spirit Mesingw.

CHAPTER 1

The Lost Boys

There was nothing to be afraid of all afternoon. The sun eased down the blue sky. The lazy hours stretched out longer and longer. For the three Lenape boys alone in the deep forest, the day seemed to last forever.

The boys chased each other down worn footpaths. They swam in a cool stream and dozed on sun-drenched rocks. They shimmied to the top of the three tallest trees they could find. Up above all the other trees, they hollered to each other and laughed, pretending to be the thunder gods who live in the clouds. It was a good day—a summer day made for adventurous boys.

They only began to think of home when the light started to fade from the sky. They started back to the village. But they had wandered farther from home than they realized. The footpaths became harder and harder to follow as late afternoon turned to dusk. Dusk gave way to evening, and before long it was so dark that the three boys were edging down the paths like old men. Soon the three boys saw no paths at all.

Branches scraped their skin as they stumbled forward in the dark. One boy thought he knew the way home, but he only led his friends deeper into the forest. The second boy thought he saw a campfire glowing in the thick woods. The boys crashed through the brush in this new direction. But they found no campfire—only the last fiery pink and orange light of the sun as it dropped behind the mountains to the west. Night fell. The three boys looked at one another but they had nothing to say. They were lost.

It was a black, moonless night. A strong wind came up and ripped through the trees. Branches snapped like twigs. The wind grew stronger. The boys feared that the wind was the giant spirit called Tornado, who walked on his hands and swept forests into the sea just by shaking his long, dark hair. Terrified, the three lost boys huddled close.

They howled in fear, but they could not hear their own cries over the roaring gusts. For a long time they simply held on to one another and wished they had stayed in the village that day.

Deep into the night the wind died down. Occasional gusts still rattled the trees, but it seemed that Tornado had passed over the three boys. In the silences between the gusts the boys' stifled sobs of relief could be heard. The wind stopped. There was silence in the forest, except for the sound of the three boys sniffling. The moon appeared from its hiding place behind the clouds. The forest filled with a silvery light. Then, one of the boys spoke. "Listen," he said.

An owl called. A woodpecker tapped an unseen tree. Somewhere, a fast-running stream chuckled. Faraway sea gulls called from where the forest met the great sea. "Listen," the boy said again. The lost boys listened. Mingled with the night sounds of the forest they heard the soft footsteps of a thousand spirits walking in the moonlight shadows. And they heard their own hearts pounding like drums.

Just before dawn, total silence fell on the forest. The boy spoke again. He pointed into the shadows. "Look," he said. His voice trembled as he spoke.

At first, the three boys thought that the figure was another lost boy. They could only see the outline of his body. He seemed as small as they were. But as the figure moved closer, they saw he had the muscles of a powerful warrior. Then he stepped into the moonlight and they saw his face.

The three boys had never seen a face more creased and wrinkled with age. The spirit was older than the oldest grandmothers and grandfathers of the village who knew every story there was to know. The spirit was as old as the forest itself.

Some Lenapes would call this spirit the Living Solid Face. Others would call him *Mesingw*—the spirit of the deer and the bear and the other animals of the forest. Mesingw would become known as a helper of lost hunters and trappers—and children lost in the forest. The first Lenapes he ever helped were the three lost boys.

Mesingw took one of the lost boys by the hand. Together, they rose into the sky. They flew to the spirit's home in the mountains of heaven above the earth. The world below glowed in the golden light of dawn. The boy could see ocean beaches and marshlands, wide rivers and rapid streams. He could see deep forests, cleared in places for crops and villages. He could see rolling green hills and high mountains with jagged, rocky peaks. He could see the great, wide homeland of his people. This was the land called *Lenapehoking*. And he could see the way back to his own village. When his flight with Mesingw was over, he confidently led his two friends home. ▲

The Lenapes believe
that the world began on
the back of a tortoise
that rose from the
ocean. The first man
and woman came from
a tree that grew on the
tortoise's back.

CHAPTER 2

The Tortoise and the Tree

The three lost boys were part of a tribe called the Lenapes. For over a thousand years the Lenapes lived and prospered on the land that the boy saw from above during his flight with Mesingw. Now known as the Middle Atlantic Coast region of the United States, it stretches from southern New York State through New Jersey, eastern Pennsylvania, and Delaware. There were about 20 different Lenape bands scattered throughout this territory. The bands belonged to the two major Lenape groups. The Munsee Lenapes inhabited the rocky highlands of the lower Hudson and upper Delaware rivers.

The Unami bands inhabited the lands around Delaware Bay in southern New Jersey, southeastern Pennsylvania, and northern Delaware. Altogether, the two groups had a population of about 24,000.

The Lenapes called their homeland Lenapehoking. It was a wilderness of thick forests, of streams and lakes and rivers, of mountains and valleys. To the east was the Atlantic Ocean. Nature was the most essential aspect of Lenape *culture* and their view of the world at large. The Lenapes saw themselves as part of nature. They were members of nature's great family. The Lenape version of the creation of the world reflects these beliefs.

According to Lenape tradition, the world began on the back of a great tortoise. The tortoise was lying in a vast ocean. Gradually, the tortoise raised his back above the water's surface. All the water ran off the tortoise, and his back became the dry earth. A tree grew in the middle of the earth. From a root of the tree grew the first man. The first man was alone (and lonely) until the tree bent over. Its top touched the ground, and another root took hold in the earth. From this root sprouted the first woman. The man was delighted.

The Lenapes performed many rituals that celebrated and strengthened their kinship with nature. Every time a Lenape baby was born, the parents of the infant placed part of the baby's *afterbirth* in the bark of a green sapling. The parents then prayed that their baby's growth would match the sapling's growth, and that both would grow up tall and strong.

The Lenapes shared a relationship with all the various parts of the natural universe. They called the sun their Elder Brother and talked of how majestic and proud he looked with his red feather headdress and yellow face paint. The moon was also a brother, as were the rain-bringing spirits called the Thunderers. The Thunderers were giant birds with human faces who shattered trees with their lightning-bolt arrows.

The four winds were thought of as the gambling grandparents. When the seasons changed, the Lenapes knew that one of the grandparents had begun to win at their game in the sky. The grandfather from the North, whom the Lenapes called "our Grandfather where it is winter," could win for several long, cold months. Then, finally, the kind spring wind would breathe across the snow-covered lands. The Lenapes would rejoice

that their "Grandmother where it is warm" was now winning the gambling game. For the Lenapes, everything in nature was alive with spiritual power, and everything in nature was part of the great family. The Lenapes were proud—but also humble—members of this family as well.

With the coming of Grandmother South Wind, many Lenapes left their smaller inland

The Lenapes who lived on the coast came together in the spring to catch fish swimming upriver.

winter communities. They traveled to large villages near rapid river mouths by the sea. In the spring, these rushing waters would be full of shad, salmon, herring, and other fish migrating upriver to *spawn*. The Lenapes captured the fish with nets and spears. Other Lenapes remained farther inland in the spring, where they gathered wild strawberries and hunted deer and bear.

In early summer, the Lenapes turned to the work of growing crops. First the men cleared plots of land with stone axes. Then they burned the fallen trees and raked the ashes into the ground to enrich the soil. In the clearings among the tree stumps, they then planted corn, squash, and beans.

As they farmed, the Lenapes offered prayers to the spirits of the crops. One of the most powerful of these spirits was the Corn Spirit. The Lenapes went to great lengths with prayers, rituals, and sacrifices to make this spirit happy so that a bountiful harvest would be ensured. When Lenape hunters returned to the villages, they would not eat the largest deer they had killed. Instead, it would be offered as a gift to their elder brother, the Corn Spirit.

Through the hot summer months the Lenape men tended their crops and pursued deer, elk, bear, turkey, and waterfowl in the lush woodlands. The women made clothing from the *tanned* hides of deer and elk. Heavy bear hides were fashioned into robes to be worn during winter. The women also fished and gathered berries and fruit.

Lenape traders traveled far and wide in the summer, sometimes all the way to the Caro-

linas and the Mississippi Valley, where they bartered with other tribes for goods. Bands of young Lenape warriors also traveled outside their homeland to raid other tribes for supplies.

When Grandmother South Wind's luck began to turn in the gambling game, cool autumn arrived. The Lenapes gathered to harvest their ripe crops. Many of these crops were dried and preserved, and then stored in the rafters of their houses or in deep bark- or mud-lined pits, to be eaten during the long, cold winter. Large tribal hunts were also organized to obtain meat to put away for the winter. Sections of forest were set on fire while hunters waited in clearings for the fleeing deer and bear to emerge. Hundreds of animals were taken in this way. The meat, as well as fish, was smoked for preservation and stored away.

The Lenapes passed the long winter months in wood-framed, bark- and grass-covered dwellings called *longhouses* and *wigwams*. As blizzards raged outside, the Lenapes stayed inside, keeping warm. The Lenapes filled the long months with conversation and stories. Traders told of the strange and distant places they had seen in their travels. Meteinuwak—Lenapes who pos-

People build a longhouse and carry out daily duties in a traditional Lenape community.

This fragment of a clay pot showing the features of a face was found in the upper Delaware valley.

sessed special spiritual powers—whispered of the even stranger lands of the supernatural beings. Young warriors bragged of their victories in battle.

Many tales were told around the fire in the longhouses and wigwams as the winter winds howled outside. Humorous tales, tales of love, and spooky tales of ghosts and magic and spirits were related. Certain tales were well known but were told again and again nevertheless. One of these was the story of the three lost boys and Mesingw. This story does not end with the three lost boys returning happily to their village in the morning. It continues to a troubled time for the people of Lenapehoking—a time of death and despair. During this time, the tribe, like the boys, becomes lost, straying far from home. And like the lost boys, it is terrorized by great and awful winds that threaten to forever scatter the Lenapes like the fallen leaves of autumn. ▲

CHAPTER 3

The Coming of the Salty Men

Many years later, Lenapes would tell the story of how the times of trouble and sorrow began. They told of a place on the other side of the world, across the great ocean. There, violent waves beat against seashore rocks. The white spray and foam from the waves formed a new kind of man. This man was not of the brown earth like the Lenapes; he was of the white of the breaking waves of the salty sea.

Ships that looked like giant sea birds resting on the water brought the salty men to the shores of Lenapehoking. The Lenapes first saw evidence of these newcomers in 1524, when the Italian *navigator* Giovanni da Verrazano sailed up the Atlantic coast. Eighty-five years later, in 1609, further contact came when the Englishman Henry Hudson sailed to inland New York State on the river later named for him. When these early explorers returned to Europe, they reported what they had seen in the New World and promised great opportunities to be had there.

Soon, Dutch, Swedish, French, and English colonists, *missionaries,* and merchants began arriving on the shores of Lenapehoking. These Europeans viewed North America as a vast new resource ready to be used to their advantage. Merchants' mouths watered at the thought of shipping cargoes of valuable animal furs back to Europe. Other Europeans dreamed of the gold, silver, and other valuable metals that might be mined from the thousands of streams and the mountains of North America. The earth itself was rich and fertile, perfect for raising crops and establishing farms.

Europeans began arriving in Lenapehoking in steadily growing numbers. Their small settlements grew into large towns and forts. The fact that the New World was already in-

Dutch, Swedish, French, and English colonists, missionaries, and merchants arrived in Lenape territory.

habited by native North Americans such as the Lenapes meant little to the Europeans, and they formed settlements wherever they wished. Except for the missionaries, who hoped to *convert* the Native Americans to

A. The Fort.
B. Church of St. Nicholas.
C. The Jail.
D. Governor's House.

NEW AMSTERDAM (NOW NEW-YORK).

As it appeared about the year 1640, while under the Dutch Government.

Christian beliefs, most Europeans viewed the Indian population as a nuisance. The Indians seemed to be a primitive, *pagan*, and inferior people. They might be useful as guides, trading partners, and laborers, but mostly the newcomers simply wanted them to disappear.

This brutal view was expressed by Johan Prinz, the powerful Swedish governor in the New World. In a letter about the Lenapes that he sent home, Prinz wrote: "Nothing would be better than to send over here a couple hundred soldiers . . . until we broke the necks of all of them. We could take possession of the places which the savages now possess."

New Amsterdam in 1640, under the Dutch government. The English later renamed the city New York.

E. *The Gallows.*
F. *The Pillory.*
G. *West India Companies Stores.*
H. *City Tavern.*

The Lenapes interacted freely with the Europeans. They were attracted by the chance to obtain items they had never had before. In exchange for animal pelts, the Lenapes received metal farming tools, axes and knives, guns, and blankets and clothing. The Lenapes also traded for objects that were less useful but attractive, such as glass beads. One item that the Lenapes traded for was neither useful nor attractive—alcohol.

The mere presence of the Europeans among the Lenapes soon proved disastrous. Along with the trading goods, the Europeans brought diseases from the Old World. The Lenapes had no natural resistance to these diseases. Soon, the tribe was ravaged by epidemics of smallpox, measles, and cholera. Fourteen deadly epidemics occurred in a 70-year period during the 1600s, and the Lenapes died by the thousands. Some Lenape communities became virtual ghost villages with a handful of stunned survivors.

It was not long before the Lenapes realized what the Europeans wanted most—Lenape lands. The Lenapes had come to depend on many of the items they obtained from the Europeans. Some Lenapes began trading rights to tribal lands to the Europeans for tools and firearms, or beads and trinkets.

Thomas West, Baron de la Warr, was the first governor of Virginia colony. The Delaware river and colony were named after him.

Others, who had become addicted to alcohol, traded away the lands of their forefathers for whiskey. A member of a rival tribe, the Iroquois, sneered at a Lenape who had been reduced to such a desperate state. After the Lenape traded away a parcel of Lenape land for a few bottles of booze, the Iroquois sneered: "This land that you claim is gone through your guts."

But not all the Lenapes parted with their homelands so easily. As more and more Europeans arrived and more towns sprang up while others grew steadily larger, hostile feelings came to the surface. By this time, the Dutch had become the most powerful European presence in Lenapehoking. Lenape warriors began speaking of driving away these invaders. In the meantime, growing numbers of Dutch soldiers were arriving in the colonial towns and villages. The Lenapes viewed their uniforms, long muskets, and shining bayonets with alarm.

By the mid-1600s, tensions between the Lenapes and the Dutch colonists were running high. Small skirmishes broke out. They were soon followed by open warfare. The smallest misunderstanding could lead to bloodshed. One war that lasted for two years was called the Peach War. It started when a

Lenape woman picked peaches on land claimed by the Dutch. The woman was shot by a colonist for her "crime." Another war erupted when a Lenape chief took a piece of tin from the Dutch fort at Swanendael, located along the South River in Delaware. The chief wanted to use the tin to make a tobacco pipe. Because the piece of tin had the Dutch battle flag imprinted on it, the chief was murdered. The Lenapes then attacked and destroyed Swanendael.

The destruction of Swanendael frightened and enraged the colonists. The Dutch governor—Governor Kieft—readied his troops. The Lenape warriors, more than prepared for a showdown, gathered from the different Lenape bands. A bitter, brutal war followed. Governor Kieft's War raged from 1640 to 1649. The Dutch army fought as if it wished to rid all Lenapes from the face of the earth. Lenape women and children were not spared. The Lenapes fought back with all the hatred for the Europeans that had been growing in their hearts.

Governor Kieft's War was soon followed by another—the Esopus War, named after the band of Munsee Lenapes who did most of the fighting. The seemingly endless warfare ravaged Lenapehoking. Thousands of Dutch and Indians were slain. Lenape villages and Dutch towns and forts were burned to the ground. The bitter fumes of battle spoiled the spring breezes of Grandmother South Wind. In autumn, Lenape prayers and sacrifices to the Corn Spirit for a bountiful harvest were replaced by mournful prayers for the dead and offerings to Ohtas, the Lenape spirit of healing. By 1864, the Lenape nation, once 24,000 strong, was near ruin from disease and war. No more than 3,000 Lenapes remained. Looking east, the despairing survivors saw the tall masts scraping the sky. The Salty Men's ships kept coming. ⧫

Penn's Treaty with
the Indians, *painted
by Benjamin West.*

CHAPTER 4

Running Away with the Land

The new wave of ships brought a different tribe of Salty Men—the British. The powerful British empire had set its sights on Lenapehoking. First, they had to defeat the Dutch. This was easily done. The long wars with the Indians had severely weakened the Dutch. By 1664, the Dutch colonial capital of New Amsterdam was under British control. The British renamed the city New York.

The British wanted the same thing the Dutch had wanted—Indian lands for colonial settlement. But the British wanted to avoid war with the Indians. They had seen from the

Indians' wars with the Dutch that large, heavily armed European armies were not guaranteed quick and easy victory over the Indians. Using what are known today as *guerrilla tactics*, the Indians had inflicted heavy damage on the Dutch armies. Their superior wilderness skills and knowledge of their home terrain had been the Lenape warriors' greatest allies. Ambushes in the deep forest, hit-and-run assaults on Dutch settlements, and the Indians' ability to move quickly and silently through the wilderness had confused and demoralized the Dutch fighters.

The cunning British moved the battle for Lenapehoking out of the forests and into colonial British courtrooms. There, Lenape leaders found themselves entangled in a web of complicated contracts, deeds to land sales, lawsuits, and "legal" claims to Lenape lands. The Lenapes soon learned that their signatures on British documents almost always meant the loss of more Lenape land, independence, and pride.

The British also forged a series of treaties with the tribes of the Northeast. This system of treaties was called the Covenant Chain. This "chain" was locked by the alliance between the British and the huge, powerful, and fierce Iroquois Nation. The battered Lenapes had no choice but to join the chain. Refusing to do so would have left them at the mercy of the Iroquois and other hostile tribes.

The Iroquois wasted no time in taking advantage of the weakened Lenapes. In 1670, the Iroquois Nation claimed authority over all the surviving Lenape bands. To the mighty Iroquois, the Lenapes seemed like pathetic weaklings fit only to be servants. Iroquois warriors called Lenape warriors "women," which to the Iroquois meant weak and inferior. The Lenapes' tribal identity—as well as their homeland—was being stripped away.

Many Lenapes, sickened by this dismal situation, began to leave Lenapehoking. Some found refuge in Moravian Protestant settlements, where they were welcomed by the kindly missionaries. These Lenapes converted to the peaceful Moravian branch of Christianity. Several Lenape bands migrated west across the Appalachian Mountains to the Ohio and Susquehanna river valleys. There, they established peaceful relations with the Miamis, Ottawas, and Shawnees. Other Lenapes headed north to Canada. In Ohio and Canada, the Lenapes entered French territory. But unlike the British and the Iroquois, the French and their Indian allies had no wish to *subjugate* the Lenapes

Etow Oh Koam, King of the River Nation. The River Nation was made up of tribes living along the Hudson River.

who came among them. Still other Lenapes simply vanished. They slipped away alone or with their families, disappearing into unknown and inaccessible places in the deep pine barrens, marshes, swamps, and mountains of the Middle Atlantic Coast. They haunted these hideaways like the Lenape *ancestral* ghosts the three lost boys heard passing through the forest during their night of terror.

Those Lenapes who remained behind did their best to survive in a world that no longer resembled the Lenapehoking of the past. Some made livings as trappers or traders. Others became *mercenary* warriors, fighting or acting as scouts for the British and their Indian allies, or the French and their Indian allies. Many Lenapes worked as servants or laborers for the colonists or the Iroquois. A meager living could be made selling herbal remedies, baskets, straw brooms, and other craft work. A few Lenapes found work on the Salty Men's whaling ships and sailed away from their people forever.

An increasing number of those Lenapes who remained adopted European ways. They lived in small, European-style houses and wore European clothing. They raised domestic livestock, such as chickens, hogs, cattle, and horses. Many planted small cornfields and apple, cherry, and peach orchards.

The Lenapes had learned to become invisible among their enemies. They had become a shadow people, expert at remaining unnoticed and avoiding confrontations with their conquerors. This ability to adapt was both a blessing and a curse. It saved the Lenapes from the complete destruction that would have resulted had they chosen to defy and fight the powerful forces that had invaded their homeland. But by giving up all resistance, the Lenapes were also giving up what little remained of their homeland. They were also in danger of forever losing their traditional tribal identity. But there were still some Lenape leaders who recognized this danger and desperately tried to prevent it.

One of these leaders was Nutimus, the chief of a large Lenape community in eastern Pennsylvania. When the British offered gold and silver for his community's lands, Nutimus refused. The land—the trees and streams and rivers and fields—was so connected to the Lenapes' self-image that to sell it would be like selling their arms and legs. Nor did Nutimus back down when threatened by the Iroquois warriors sent by the British to intimidate him. The British were forced to use trickery to knock the stubborn leader from the land of his ancestors.

The 1736 Walking Purchase, as it was later to be called, began when James Logan, a colonial lawyer, produced a suspicious-looking copy of a 1684 contract that gave the British the rights to the land Nutimus refused to sell. Logan claimed that the original con-

The Lenapes lost their legal claim of land to the British by signing British deeds, or bills of sale.

tract had been destroyed in a fire. Nutimus was well aware of the British history of shady dealings with the Indians. He resisted Logan's pressure to sign a confirmation of the contract. Logan claimed that Nutimus had no voice in the matter. He pointed out that the chief had been born a few miles from the land in question. Nutimus replied by asking the white man how *he* had come "to have a right here, as he was not born in this country?"

Unfortunately, other Lenapes living on those lands, tempted by gold or frightened by Iroquois threats, began to sign the contract. Piece by piece, the British obtained the land. To stop this gradual bleeding away of the land, Nutimus made a deal with the British.

He would sell to the British as much land as they could walk across in one and a half days. After that, the British agreed to stop harassing his tribe and leave them in peace.

In past land transactions of this sort, the boundaries were always paced off slowly. The walkers were expected to "rest and smoke along the way." Nutimus signed the contract believing that this tradition would be upheld. Logan made sure that it was not. First he employed an army of surveyors to find the route that would encompass the most land. Then woodsmen cut a path through the thick forest along this route.

At sunrise on the chosen day, three long-distance runners took off down the cleared trail. They ran so hard that two of them dropped from exhaustion. The third runner, followed by a horse-drawn cart filled with food and water to keep him strong, finished the mission. When the day and a half was over, he had run away with all the remaining Lenape land in eastern Pennsylvania. Lenape migration west increased dramatically.

By the middle of the 18th century, the Lenapes had all but abandoned Lenapehoking. The last Lenape leader to offer resistance was Pisquetomen. In the Lenape language, Pisquetomen means "he that keeps on though it is getting dark." Pisquetomen

continued on page 49

SIGNS OF A CHANGING CULTURE

Originally an East Coast Indian tribe, the Lenapes were driven westward as the Europeans took over their land, called Lenapehoking. Because of their relocation, the Lenapes had to adjust to new environments, neighbors, and a new way of life. The Lenapes expressed these changes in the objects they made.

When the Lenapes moved to Indiana in the early 1800s, they did not have the wealth to practice all of their ancient religious celebrations. Instead, they combined their many ceremonies into one—Xingwikaon (Big House). For this annual festivity, the Lenapes made objects such as mesingw masks, turtle-shell rattles, and drums.

As the Lenapes moved farther west, the methods and styles of decoration reflected their new environment. Indians of the Great Plains taught them to make jewelry from silver, and the Lenapes excelled at the new art. Instead of the colorfully dyed porcupine quills the Lenapes had used for decoration in the East, they began to use glass beads and bright abstract designs similar to those of their new Indian neighbors.

A Lenape wooden flute, dating from the late 19th or early 20th century.

A carved wooden mask of a *mesingw*, or game spirit, worn by a dancer in the Big House ceremony.

A Big House prayerstick, topped by a mesingw head and strung with metal chimes and janglers.

A Big House rattle, made from the shell of a box turtle and filled with bits of marine shell.

A Big House drum and drumsticks carved with mesingw. The faces have been hewn so that they look toward the drummer.

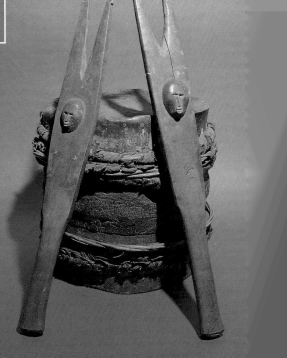

Lenape silver armbands, probably from the late 19th century. Such items were introduced to North America by non-Indian settlers in the 1600s but were later made by Indians.

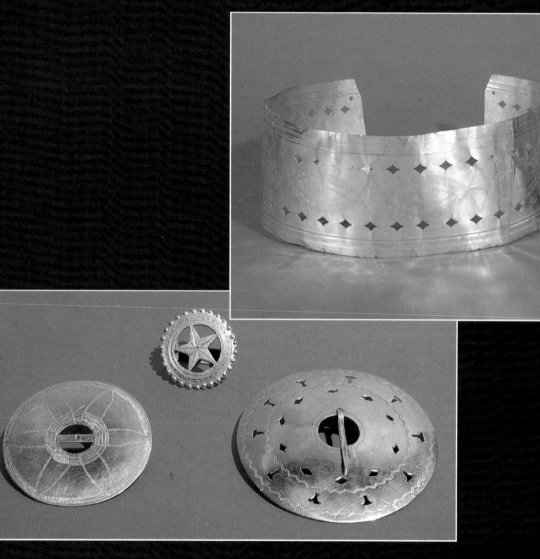

Silver brooches were worn by Lenape women to adorn their cotton dresses, which gradually replaced traditional animal skin clothing.

Hair ornaments such as this were worn by Lenape men in the West. Feathers or ribbons were attached to the small wand, which protruded from the hair.

Three bracelets and a ring crafted in the late 19th century by a skilled Lenape silversmith.

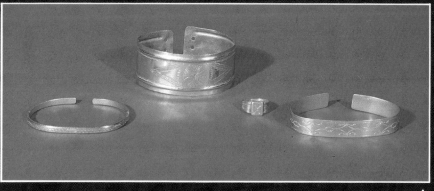

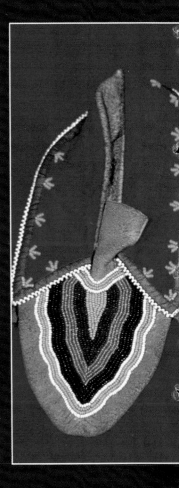

A Delaware shirt adorned with beads in designs much like those used by tribes native to the Midwest.

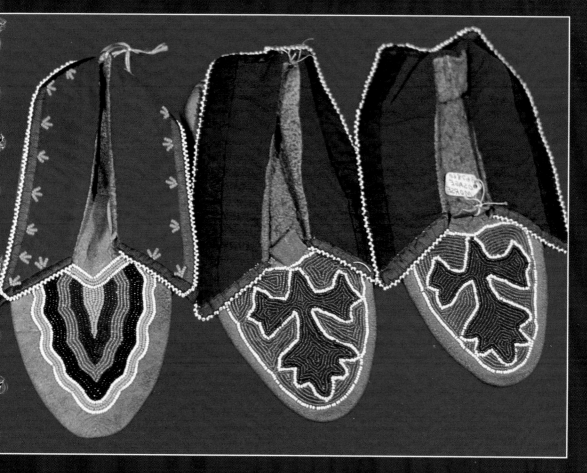

Colorful, abstract beadwork patterns decorate the tops and flaps of these Delaware moccasins from the early 20th century.

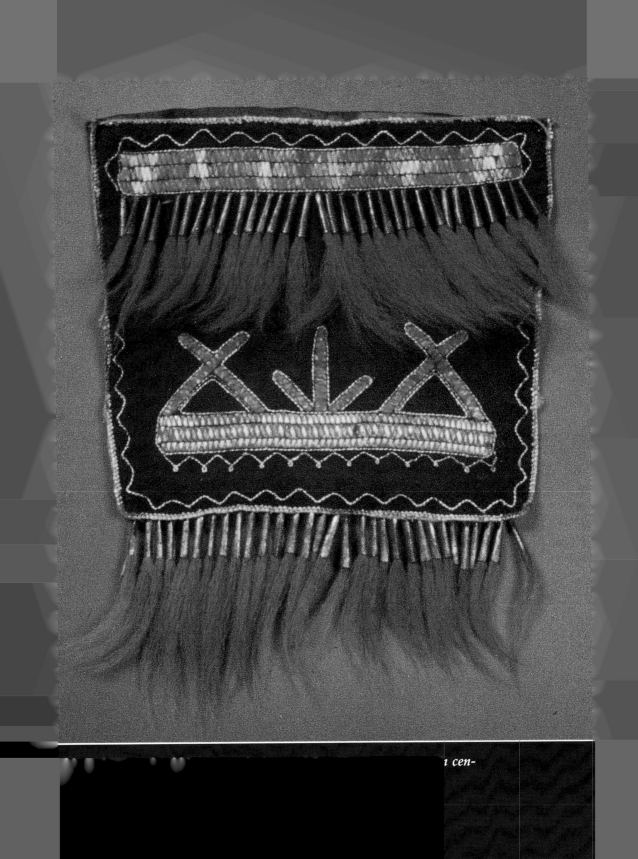

cen-

continued from page 40

refused to accept the dismal situation into which the Lenapes had fallen. His cries for rebellion and his outright hatred for the colonists awoke deep feelings in many Lenapes. There was talk of an uprising against the colonists and their allies. But the British, aware of the young warrior's defiant attitude, lost no time in threatening most Lenapes into withdrawing support for Pisquetomen.

Powerless in his own homeland, Pisquetomen joined the *exodus* to the lands in the Ohio and Susquehanna river valleys, beyond the Appalachian Mountains. Leaving behind the lands that Mesingw had shown to the lost boys during their magical flight, Pisquetomen, followed by many of the last Lenapes, journeyed west toward the setting sun. True to his name, Pisquetomen traveled on through the darkness. ▲

A 1768 map of northern
colony boundaries set
by the Indians and the
British in the Treaty of
Fort Stanwix.

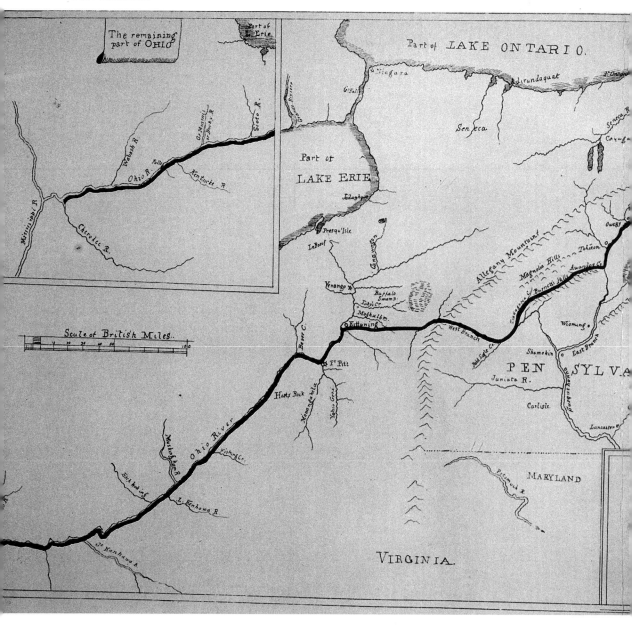

MAP
the FRONTIERS of the
RTHERN COLONIES
the BOUNDARY LINE established
on them and the Indians at the Treaty
y Sr Will Johnson at F^t Stanwix in Nov^r
1768.
cted and Improved from Evans Map,
By Guy Johnson Dep Ag^t of Ind Affairs

CHAPTER 5

"These Dogs Clothed in Red"

The tribe of the lost boys had itself become lost.

The Lenapes now lived in exile, far from Lenapehoking. Many of them had scattered to unknown parts and faraway lands. Others now gathered in the Susquehanna River valley in western Pennsylvania. There, they found refuge among the Shawnees and Nanticokes. Farther west, in Ohio, Lenapes settled among the Miamis and Wyandots.

The three lost boys had survived their night of fear and despair by clinging together against the terrible wind. Eventually, they were helped by a member of the spirit world—Mesingw. Now the remaining Lenapes, blown far from home, clung together to survive. And soon, they, too, were assisted by the spirits.

The Lenape prophet Neolin was a meteinuwak, a tribal doctor or medicine man. The message he brought from the spirit world was simple but powerful: cast off the ways of the white man and return to the ways of the Lenape ancestors. Then the Great Spirit would rid them of their white enemy. Neolin went so far as to encourage the Indians to give up their weapons, however, which left those that followed him unprotected.

Other Lenape leaders, such as Shingas, Beaver, and Netawatwees, began calling the Lenape bands together. In 1755, these bands formed the Delaware nation. They declared that the Delawares were an independent people. They would be ruled by no one—not the British or the Iroquois or anyone else. What had begun as a retreat and exile now became a gathering of strength.

War for control of the Northeast was brewing between the two major European powers—Britain and France. The Delawares allied themselves with the French. Unlike the British, the French treated the Indians with respect. And they hated the British as much as the Delawares did. Now, armed with French guns and supplies, and a renewed sense of tribal identity and pride, the Delawares prepared for war. The time for vengeance had arrived.

The British were confident that their superior military strength would make quick work of the French. Fearlessly, they sent an invasion force into southwestern Pennsylvania. Their aim was to attack the French stronghold of Fort Duquesne (now the city of Pittsburgh). The leader of the British force was General Edward Braddock. Braddock arrogantly dismissed the French and their allies as nothing more than "a few naked Indians and Canadians." Then the French and their new allies struck the first blow.

On the morning of July 9, 1755, Braddock led 1,500 troops through the Pennsylvania woodlands toward Fort Duquesne. The forest shadows cloaked a waiting band of French, Delaware, and Shawnee fighters. As Braddock's army crossed the Monongahela River, about 9 miles from Fort Duquesne, they were ambushed. The peace of the forest was abruptly shattered by shrill war cries, and from the shadows poured a deadly rain of bullets, arrows, spears, and tomahawks. The bewildered British soldiers

Delaware chief
Teedyuscung, who
took over leadership
as the war against
the English began.

fired wildly into the trees as their fellow soldiers fell by the dozens. Soon they were running in outright panic. General Braddock, mortally wounded, was dragged away by a young officer named George Washington. As he sat propped against a tree, the dying Braddock asked again and again in stunned disbelief: "Who would have thought it? Who would have thought it?"

The Delawares were just getting started. Now they waged war against the British and the colonists with a rage that had been building for decades. Pisquetomen took his place as leader of the Delawares. Along with Shawnee and Wyandot allies, Pisquetomen's warriors raided farms and homesteads as far east as New Jersey. Farms and houses burned, and hundreds of white settlers were slain. Terrified white settlers in the Ohio River valley and western Pennsylvania fled eastward toward the safety of British forts.

In 1758, the Iroquois approached the Delawares, expecting them to accept an offer of peace. A Delaware chief told the Iroquois to get off of Delaware land. "We are men," the Delaware leader declared, "and are determined not to be ruled any longer by you as women."

Despite the ferocity of their campaign, as the war dragged on the Delawares and their allies began to lose ground. Even as French support dwindled, the Delawares still fought on. Soon, however, many war-weary Delawares came to believe that they were fighting a losing battle. They had lost many warriors who could not be replaced. But no matter how many white men they killed or captured, the enemy kept coming in greater numbers.

In 1756, the influential Delaware leader Teedyuscung stepped into the fray. Along with many of his tribespeople, Teedyuscung had converted to Christianity among the Moravians. These Delawares, following the teachings of the Moravians, were nonviolent. They had remained *neutral* throughout the war. Acting as a peacemaker and *diplomat*, Teedyuscung convinced the Delawares to meet with the British to discuss terms of peace.

In 1758, in the town of Easton, Pennsylvania, the Delawares and the British signed a peace treaty. The English brought many gifts. They promised to protect the Delawares from hostile tribes, to return all prisoners, to establish fair trade relations with the Delawares, to take no more of their lands, and to provide financial compensation for the loss of Lenapehoking. For their part, the Delawares promised to return prisoners, to stop helping the French, to end hostilities against the British army and the colonists, and to provide British troops with safe passage through their lands.

Now that they were able to move safely through Delaware territory, the British quickly gained the upper hand against the French. By 1763, they had driven the French from eastern North America. The long and bloody French and Indian War was over. But to the dismay of the Delawares and the other tribes living west of the Appalachians, for the British "safe passage" through the Indians' territories had now become permanent occupation. The British army, which had flooded into the territory in great numbers following the Easton Treaty, showed no signs of departing now that they had beaten the French. Instead, the British leaders announced that their troops would remain permanently to "protect" the Indians.

This would not do. The Delawares and the other tribes in that region had seen quite enough of the British. The Delawares were ready to take up the fight again, but the war and new epidemics had reduced their army to a mere 500 warriors. There were thousands of British troops in the region. But the other tribes scattered throughout the Ohio River valley region were ready to come to the

aid of the Delawares. All the tribes united behind the great Ottawa warrior-chief, Pontiac. Traveling from village to village, Pontiac spoke to the different tribes about the presence of the red-uniformed British troops. "Drive off your land these dogs clothed in red," Pontiac urged. "They will do you nothing but harm."

Pontiac's bands of warriors launched a series of lightning attacks against the British.

Angry colonists known as the Paxton Boys murdered peaceful Indians in Harrisburg, Pennsylvania, in 1763. They attacked the Indians in retaliation for the killing of settlers by the Delawares.

In the winter of 1763, the Indians hit British outposts and forts throughout the lands west of the Appalachians. By summer, Pontiac's forces had destroyed all but two strongly defended British strongholds—Fort Detroit and Fort Pitt. These final two British footholds were both attacked and surrounded by Delaware, Shawnee, and Ottawa forces. But the British managed to hold off Pontiac's warriors throughout the summer. In August, British reinforcements arrived. Pontiac sent a large force to stop the British column heading toward Fort Pitt. On August 5 and 6, about 30 miles from the fort, the two armies clashed. When the bloody fight—which came to be known as the Battle of Bushy Run—was over, the British were victorious. Fort Pitt was relieved days later. In November, Fort Detroit was retaken by the British.

Pontiac's Rebellion was failing. Now the Britons and the colonists took a fearful revenge on the Indians. Bands of colonial *militia* slaughtered Indians wherever they found them. Even peaceful Indians, who had taken no part in the uprising, were massacred. Teedyuscung, the wise and peace-loving Delaware diplomat, was murdered. Fresh British troops *rampaged* through the Ohio River valley. Indian settlements were overrun and burned to the ground. The

CHIEF WHITE EYES

LENAPE "INDIAN" CHIEF AND U.S. LIEUTENANT COLONEL COQUETAKEGHTON IN THE AMERICAN REVOLUTION · SAUTS

Delawares made a final stand at Coshocton, their major settlement, in November 1764. The settlement was taken easily by the British, and the Delawares surrendered.

The especially harsh Treaty of Fort Stanwix, signed near Oneida Lake in New York State, stripped the Delawares of all the lands they had retaken during Pontiac's Rebellion.

White Eyes, chief of the Delaware nation. In 1774 he signed the first treaty between an Indian tribe and the 13 colonies that would become the United States.

Those Delawares who had survived the wars retired to settlements in eastern Ohio. By 1770, almost all of the remaining Delawares were living in Newcomer's Town near the Tuscarawas River. Many of the war-weary Delawares embraced Moravian Christianity, with its emphasis on charity and non-violence. In Newcomer's Town, the Delawares led a quiet existence. They built small log houses along tidy streets and raised crops on small plots of land. Other nearby tribes, respectful of the Delawares' long suffering and their quiet, survivors' wisdom, called them the Grandfathers. Even young Delawares seemed to carry a sorrowful, elderly wisdom in their eyes. Green Lenapehoking, with its deep, shadowy forests, its clear, cold rivers and streams, and its many spirits, now existed only in tales told by elders.

The peaceful times at Newcomer's Town did not last. The Delawares seemed caught up in an endless cycle of war and exile. In 1776, the American Revolution broke out. Again, the Delawares were drawn into the fighting, although the Moravian Delawares remained *aloof*. In a strange twist of history, most of the Delawares eventually sided with the British and their Iroquois allies in the struggle. At the outset, they favored the

cause of the rebellious colonies, but two incidents of treachery and murder turned them against the colonists. The Delawares found themselves fighting alongside their traditional tormentors, the British and the Iroquois.

The first incident occurred in 1778 when shortly after the Delaware chief White Eyes

Buckongahelas led Delaware and Shawnee warriors in raids on frontier settlements in the late 18th century. The war leader is drawn here with a mesinghholikan dancer.

signed a treaty of alliance with the 13 colonies, he was murdered by colonial frontiersmen. The second incident happened in March 1782, when the 90 men, women, and children of Gnadenhutten, a peaceful Moravian settlement, were slaughtered by colonial militiamen. The Moravian Delawares sang Christian hymns and prayers as they were massacred.

Incidents such as these turned the majority of Delawares against the colonists. When the British lost the war and withdrew from North America, the Delawares continued to fight the Americans.

Led by the warrior Buckongahelas, they waged war for two more years until a peace treaty was signed in 1785. The treaty moved the Delawares farther west into Ohio. Soon after, white settlers demanded that all Indian tribes be removed from Ohio.

The Indians did not go peacefully. Thirty-five tribes in the region, including the Delawares, formed a confederacy. Led by the Miami chief Little Turtle, with Buckongahelas by his side, they prepared for the American troops. When the troops came, Little Turtle's forces were ready. In 1790, the Indians turned back an army of 1,500 American soldiers. A year later, the Indians inflicted a savage beating on an army of 2,000 sent into

Miami war chief Little Turtle led Indians in defeating two armies of Americans in the 1790s. The third American army triumphed over the Indians.

Ohio. Little Turtle's warriors virtually wiped out the American force. But the Americans kept coming. A third army, led by the revolutionary war hero General "Mad Anthony" Wayne, finally defeated the Indian confederacy at Fallen Timbers in 1794.

The following year, a peace conference was held at Fort Greenville. The Americans knew that the Delawares were beaten once and for all when Buckongahelas strode into the room. The fearless warrior layed his war tomahawk on the table. "All who know me," he announced, "know me as a man and a warrior." The Delaware chief then vowed to fight no more. ▲

A painting of Shawnee prophet Tenskwatawa in the early 1800s. He encouraged his followers to believe that Europeans were evil and should be killed for witchcraft.

CHAPTER **6**

"Let Us Hope"

Once again the Delawares were uprooted. They were pushed farther west, to Indiana. A deep despair settled over the tribe as the 19th century dawned. There were fewer and fewer Delawares. A century and a half of war, sickness, defeat, and exile had taken its toll. The past was a bitter memory. The future seemed to hold little hope. It seemed that the spirits had abandoned the Delawares. They no longer felt like members of the great family of nature and the universe. Instead, they viewed themselves as outcasts.

A wise, elderly Delaware woman named Beate believed that her tribe had to return to its traditional ways in order to save itself. She advised the Delawares to reject the white man and his ways. She encouraged the Delawares to appeal to the ancient spirits of Lenapehoking, who had protected and nurtured the Lenapes in their long-lost homeland.

"Build a house," Beate instructed. "Use only natural materials, as our Lenape ancestors did. Do not use glass windows, iron nails, or any other European materials. Build a house where the old spirits may gather and be honored. This is how the spirits will come. If you do what I have told you," Beate promised, "they will once more come out."

The Delawares built the house as Beate instructed. It was called the Xingwikaon, or Big House. The four walls of the house symbolized the four grandparent winds. The dirt floor was the turtle's back, which was the earth. The ceiling was the heavenly home of Kishelemukong—the creator of all things. The Milky Way swirled on the oval dance floor, and earth and heaven touched through the Big House's center post. On this post was a carving of the Living Solid Face—Mesingw.

Beate's Big House became the center of a Delaware spiritual renewal. Every October, the Delawares would hold a 12-day Big

House ceremony. The ceremony filled the Big House with the spirits of Lenapehoking. During the ceremony, the Big House resounded with traditional songs, chants, prayers, and dances. A step through its doors was a step into a forgotten time. The air in the Big House seemed crowded with spirits. Red cedar was burned to purify the air and to carry prayers to Kishelemukong.

Word of the spiritual revival led by Beate attracted many Delawares who had scattered following the war with the Americans. Delawares from small *reservations* in upper New York State, Long Island, Massachusetts, and New Jersey traveled to Indiana to reunite their tribe. At the same time, however, thousands of white settlers were flooding into Indiana. The Delawares, who grew to number 3,000 at the most, were helpless to resist. A final *dispersal* of the tribe was set in motion. Many Delawares were forced westward once again, to Missouri, Kansas, and Oklahoma. Some ended up in Arkansas and Texas. Others headed north to Wisconsin and Canada.

The centuries of hardship that followed the arrival of the Salty Men on the shores of Lenapehoking had broken apart the Lenapes. But they had also taught the tribe how to adapt and survive. And that is what the scattered pockets of Lenapes, known as absentee Delawares, continued to do. Those who found themselves in the Great Plains region learned how to hunt buffalo like the Plains Indians. Delaware trappers journeyed all the way to the Rocky Mountains for beaver. Delaware farmers took to raising horses, cattle, sheep, and hogs, and soon earned a reputation for the high quality of their livestock. The Delawares also excelled as trackers and guides. Black Beaver, James Secondine, and John C. Connor were among the Delawares who used their wilderness skills to help guide explorers and naturalists such as John C. Frémont and James Audubon.

But the hardships and sorrows continued. *Predatory* Indian tribes and hostile settlers persecuted the Delawares. U.S. government policies made it virtually impossible for them to settle together on decent land. As the 20th century began, the Delawares no longer existed as a tribe. Small pockets of Delawares tried to keep alive the teachings of Beate, but white American culture was stronger magic. The last Big House ceremony was held in Copan, Oklahoma, in 1924.

The Delawares, many of them homeless and poverty stricken, began to believe that their best chance for survival was to adapt themselves to white American ways. Young Delawares left the small communities to attend white schools or find employment in the cities. Many of them never returned. Others joined the armed forces and died in foreign lands fighting for the government that had persecuted their people. As the older generations died off, the Lenape languages and traditional ways died with them.

But some members of the tribe refused to allow their precious tribal heritage to fade quietly away. One of these tribespeople was Nora Thompson Dean, whose Delaware name meant "Touching Leaves Woman." Dean was born at the turn of the century, when the government was enforcing a policy of sending Indian children to white schools. She quickly realized that she would have to fight to hold on to her Indian heritage. She refused the government teacher's modern lessons. For her, the sun was still an elder brother, and the spring wind a grandmother, and the stars were still the footprints of her deceased ancestors. Even the land, which the United States now owned from coast to coast, was still for her the shell of the giant turtle that had risen from the waters to form the sacred earth. Dean had listened closely

Delaware leaders perform a reburial ceremony for human remains found on Ellis Island, New York, in 1987. Some traditions remain with the Indians today.

to the stories of her surviving tribal elders, and she would not forget them. Instead, she began telling them to other Delawares whenever and wherever she could.

Over the years, Dean's reputation as a storyteller spread. Delawares gathered at her Indian crafts store in Oklahoma to hear her tales. They were followed by white historians and *anthropologists*. Dean received special honors from the governors of Oklahoma, Pennsylvania, and Delaware. The honors mattered little to Dean. What was important to her was to pass on the traditions of her tribe to the younger generations.

She was not alone in this task. Other traditionalists, such as Charley Elkhair, Jonathan "Charley" Weber, and Nathan Montour, strove to keep alive the customs of the past. It was never easy, and sometimes even these tribespeople despaired that they were fighting yet another losing battle. When Nathan Montour was near his death, he told a white scholar his bleak view of the future: "I have become convinced that when the older people of this generation pass away there will be no one left that will be able to relate the traditions and cultures of the past . . . as the younger generations couldn't care less." At Montour's funeral, a prayer was said by Nora Thompson Dean. The prayer was in Montour's Delaware dialect. No one in the room could understand a word.

A few years later, in 1984, Dean followed Montour up into the Milky Way along the trail of stars left by her departed ancestors. At her funeral, Lucy Parks Blalock, one of the few Lenapes who could still speak the old language of Lenapehoking, offered this simple prayer: "Kwela apchichwemi awen mevashalawoo yak Lenapeyok." "Let us hope the Lenape will be remembered forever."▲

GLOSSARY

afterbirth   the placenta and membranes that hold a fetus during pregnancy and are discharged minutes after the baby's birth; in some cultures thought to be a very powerful substance

aloof   removed or distant in interest or involvement; disinterested

ancestral   relating to or inherited from ancestors (persons from whom one is descended, or, long-ago creators of a group of people: a family, tribe, race, or other)

anthropologist   a scientist who studies the origin, environment, social relations, and culture of human beings

convert   to change from one belief to another

culture   the traditions, art, spiritual beliefs, language, and way of life of a people

diplomat   a person who peacefully conducts negotiations between two parties, such as two nations

dispersal   the act of breaking up a unit and spreading it widely, even to the point of vanishing

exodus   the departure of a large group; emmigration

guerrilla tactics   irregular combat by independent military groups, including such techniques as harassment, hit-and-run attack and retreat, and sabotage

Lenapehoking   the Delaware name for the Lenape homeland; literally means "the land of the people"

longhouse   a large, bark-covered dwelling that housed several Lenape families

mercenary   one who is paid to serve in a foreign army

mesingw   spirits of the game animals that the Indians hunted; also, the name of the spirit who would help lost hunters, trappers, and children

militia	part of a nation's armed forces called upon in case of emergency
missionary	a person who tries to teach others about his or her religion with the goal of converting them
navigator	one who steers a way from place to place, usually on board a ship
neutral	not taking part on either side
pagan	one who believes in a number of related gods, or a person who has little or no religion and is attached to worldly pleasures
predatory	showing an inclination toward injuring or using others for personal gain
rampage	to act along a course of wildly violent and riotous behavior
reservation	an area of land designated by the U.S. government, within which Indian tribes were forcibly settled
spawn	to produce offspring
subjugate	to bring under control; conquer
tan	to turn animal hides into leather
wigwam	a one-room, cone-shaped dwelling made of saplings or branches covered with mats or birch bark

CHRONOLOGY

1524   Lenapes encounter first white men when Giovanni da Verrazano sails up the Atlantic coast

1609   Henry Hudson sails to inland New York State; Europeans begin arriving in Lenape territory in growing numbers

1630–1767   Lenapes sign nearly 800 deeds, giving most of Lenapehoking to the Europeans

1640–64   The Peach War, Governor Kieft's War, and the Esopus War—against the Dutch—take many Lenape lives

1664   The Dutch colonial capital of New Amsterdam comes under British control and is renamed New York

1670   The Iroquois Nation claims authority over all surviving Lenape bands

1736   Lenapes sign the Walking Purchase, which takes away their claim to land in eastern Pennsylvania

1755   Lenapes and their French allies battle with the British; Lenape bands come together to form the Delaware Nation

1758   The Delawares and the British sign a peace treaty at Easton, Pennsylvania

1763   The British drive the French out of eastern North America

1763–64   Pontiac's Rebellion against the British

1764   The Delawares surrender to the British at the Indian settlement Coshocton, Ohio

1768   The Treaty of Fort Stanwix forces the Delawares to move north with the Iroquois or west to Ohio

1776   The American Revolution breaks out, and Delawares are drawn into fighting

1778   Delaware chief White Eyes signs a treaty of alliance with the 13 colonies and is murdered

1782   Colonial militiamen slaughter the inhabitants of a peaceful Moravian Delaware settlement

1785 Peace treaty signed between Americans and Delawares, moving the Delawares farther west

1790–91 Miami war chief Little Turtle successfully leads a confederacy of Indian tribes, including many Delaware, against the Americans

1794 Indian confederacy decisively defeated at Fallen Timbers, Ohio

1795 Peace treaty between Indian confederacy and Americans signed at Fort Greenville, Ohio; all Delaware land in Ohio is given up to Americans

1818–40 Remaining Delawares move to Indiana, are forced out by white settlers, and move farther west and north, separating the tribe forever

1924 Last performance of the Big House ceremony, during which all the spirits of the Lenape homeland are called through traditional songs, chants, prayers, and dances

1984 Famous Delaware storyteller and traditionalist Norma Thompson Dean dies, leaving only a handful of people who know any of the Delaware languages; Delaware leaders perform reburial rites for human remains found on Ellis Island in New York

INDEX

ABOUT THE AUTHOR

JOSH WILKER is a writer living in Brooklyn, New York. He is the author of a forthcoming biography of Julius Erving.

PICTURE CREDITS